Rebecca's REWARD

Written by
Valerie Miller

Illustrated by
Charity Miller

Happy 6th Birthday
Rebekah!

Love You Forever!

Papa & Nana
XOXOXO

ISBN: 978-1-943929-24-5

Cover design and layout: Kristi Yoder

Printed in the USA

Second printing: September 2021

Published by:
TGS International
P.O. Box 355
Berlin, Ohio 44610 USA
Phone: 330-893-4828
Fax: 330-893-4893
www.tgsinternational.com

Two bright eyes looked out from under a bush at the edge of the porch. The eyes were watching a little girl as she stepped outside and looked around, searching for something. She stood still for a bit. Then she saw those bright, eager eyes looking at her.

"Come, Sheba, let's go get the cows!" Rebecca exclaimed, and the black and white dog scrambled out of its shady napping spot under the bush. The dog's brown eyes looked enthusiastic about fetching the cows.

Rebecca slipped out the lane behind the barn. Bringing the cows in from the pasture at four o'clock every afternoon was her own special chore. Often her younger brother Daniel helped, and Sheba always helped.

Sheba was such a good dog. She was gentle with little children. Whenever a car came into the driveway, she would bark a little to announce that somebody was coming. Then she wagged her tail to welcome the visitors.

Sheba helped Daddy by hunting woodchucks in the fields and

woods. Woodchucks dug holes in the fields, and sometimes the hay mower would hit one of their holes and break. Daddy was always glad to hear that Sheba had caught a woodchuck.

Rebecca saw the cows at the far end of the pasture, in the nice shade beside the stream. She rounded up the cows farthest away, flapping her barn apron to get them moving.

"Don't loiter," Mom had told her before she left the house. "Daddy is in a hurry to milk, and I need your help as soon as you come back."

The cows all headed to the stream for a drink. The stream came from a big pond along one side of the cow pasture, flowing out of a narrow place under some trees. Then it leaped and splashed down a waterfall, around some rocks, and into a little pond. Wild ducks often paddled among the cattails in the little pond, and blue herons stood stock still on tall legs, waiting for fish to come close enough to grab with their long, pointed beaks.

Rebecca loved to play here. Minnows hid in the little pools, just waiting to be caught and put into another pool. The waterfall was like a slippery stair to climb up and down, and there were plenty of stones to make dams and walkways.

Quietly, Rebecca waded across the stream to the other side. There she spied a frog in a clump of grass and grabbed it with both hands. It wriggled and squirmed, and she peeked between her fingers to look at it. Then she slowly uncovered the frog and held him out over the water. He sat there for just a second before making a flying leap and a delightful splash!

Suddenly Rebecca remembered the cows. They had all finished drinking and were spread out across the meadow.

"Get up, cows," she called, splashing out of the stream. They'd better hurry now! "Move along there, Muffin, Creamy! Get up, Bessie!" The cows started walking along the narrow cow paths and tramped single file toward the barn, Rebecca behind them. Up ahead she saw her favorite apple tree amid the row of old, crooked apple trees. Were the apples ripening? She would quickly climb one branch of the split trunk and see. Mmm . . . how good the sugar-sweet apples would taste! But they weren't ripe yet.

Remembering the cows, she jumped down and ran to catch up with them. Suddenly she felt a painful sting on her toe. She sat down with a bump. She had stepped on a bee! Pulling up her foot, she scratched where she had been stung. Then she hurried the cows to the barn. She deserved the bee sting, she knew. Mom had told her not to loiter.

As Mom mixed vinegar and baking soda in a cup and spread it over the bee sting, she reminded Rebecca that God always sees when we do wrong. "Do you think God sent the bee to remind you to obey my instructions?" Mom asked.

Rebecca was ashamed. A seven-year-old girl is old enough to remember to do as her mother says. She determined to try harder to obey.

Diligent. Rebecca liked the sound of the word. It sounded grown-up. Like making cheese all by herself. Or like having a pet that she was responsible for.

The cheese curds were heated to just the right temperature. Mom stopped stirring and turned the burner off. She got her big stainless steel strainer and set it on the counter. Then she unfolded a cheesecloth and laid it over the top of the strainer. The cheesecloth was a special one. A pattern of squares was woven into it. It was not meant to be a cheesecloth at all, but Mom had needed a new one. When she was shopping at a store, she noticed this white, airy cotton fabric, and she thought, *I could hem the edges to make a perfectly good cheesecloth, and it would cost less than buying a specially made one!* So that was what she did, and the new cloth did work every bit as good as real cheesecloth. It even left faint, pretty squares pressed into the cheese from the woven pattern on the cloth.

"Now, Rebecca, you may dry the dishes and put them away, and I will scrub potatoes for lunch while we wait for the curds to settle," Mom said. "Daniel may bring a bucket from the porch to put the whey into."

Rebecca was thinking while she carefully dried each dish and put it where it belonged. She thought, *I would very much like to someday have an animal all my own. But I'm quite sure it will never happen if I'm not diligent. I must try hard to do my work well.* Playing around when she should be bringing in the cows certainly was not being diligent. Neither would it be diligent to leave a few dishes in the drainer so she could go watch the cheese being ladled into the strainer. She quickly dried the last cups and skipped over to where Daniel was calling for her to help hold up the corners of the cheesecloth. The cloth-lined strainer was not big enough to hold all the curds, so Daniel and Rebecca each held up two corners of the cheese-cloth and Mom poured in the last curds. Then Mom gathered all the corners of the cloth and tied them together. Whey drained from the ball of cheese. Mom wrapped a heavy

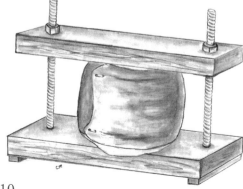

band of cloth around and around it. Then she put the cheese ball in the press and screwed down the top board.

"You haven't said a word since you started drying the dishes." Mom smiled at Rebecca. "What's on your mind?"

"I was wishing I could have an animal all my own," Rebecca explained. "One that likes me better than anyone else. Do you think that will ever happen?"

Mom understood. Rebecca was thinking of the calf story and wanting to become diligent so that she, too, could be rewarded with a pet.

"Diligence has its own rewards. The satisfaction of a job done right gives a happy feeling," Mom told her. "Often there is no other reward for work well done. When we have done our best, we know God is pleased, and He gives us a happy heart.

"Once in a while we may get some unexpected blessing, but it is enough to know that we've put forth our best efforts and our work is well done. I don't know if you will someday receive a pet for your own or not," said Mom. "But I'm sure you will discover that if you are diligent, you will be rewarded with happiness, and others will trust you with bigger responsibilities. Remember the verse I talked about?"

Rebecca nodded. She repeated it out loud. " 'He that is faithful in that which is least is faithful also in much.' "

"If you try hard now, you'll get into a good habit," Mom said. "Then when you're grown up, you'll still be diligent because that's what you're used to doing!"

3

Daddy's cheerful whistle echoed off the milk house walls as he scrubbed out the milk tank. Daddy could whistle better than anyone else Rebecca knew. She had tried and tried to form her mouth like his when he whistled, and sometimes she could make a little sound, but not pretty songs like Daddy's. His whistle bounced up and down, as clear as a bird's song.

"Mom and Sarah are coming now," Rebecca called from the doorway where she was watching. "We can go unload hay."

It was haymaking time. Three big wooden wagons were full of hay bales, and everyone was needed to get the hay stored in the haymow. They all liked haymaking time. Daddy and Mom were glad because they would have hay in the barn for the cows to eat next winter. Rebecca, Daniel, and Sarah were glad because it was fun to roll the bales from the top of the wagon down to the floor where Daddy put them on the conveyor.

Daddy started the tractor and parked the wagon beside the conveyor. Daniel climbed up to the top of the load where the breeze ruffled his hair, but Rebecca stepped up on a bale by the barn wall where she could reach the conveyor switches. She and Daniel must take turns rolling bales to Daddy and watching the switches. It was not fun to watch the switches, but Daddy said it was an important job because if a bale got stuck and the conveyor was not turned off in time, something might break. So Rebecca watched the switches for one load of bales, then Daniel took a turn for the next load. Sarah was not yet tall enough to reach the switches.

One at a time, Daddy dropped the bales on the clattering conveyor. It carried the bales up, up almost to the roof. There the bales bounced onto a short conveyor that went through the big opening inside the haymow. Then a long conveyor took the bales smoothly to the other end of the haymow, where it dumped them off on a pile. No one could see inside the haymow from the wagon where they were working, so Mom's job was to climb into the haymow and watch that everything kept working properly in there. If the conveyor stalled or a bale got jammed, she would pound three times on the tin barn wall. *Bang! Bang! Bang!* meant "Turn the switches off quickly!" When everything was fixed up again, all the switches could be turned back on and the bales continued on their journey to the big pile at the other end of the haymow.

When all the hay was unloaded, the children climbed into the wagon while Daddy drove out the field lane to the hayfield. There, puttering along in first gear, they pushed all the loose

hay off the wagon into a windrow. Daddy would hook up to the baler again and bale this last, loose hay.

When it was time to bring the cows in from the pasture, Daniel took Jenny, the goat, along. It was so hard to keep Jenny inside a fence so she had to stay in the barn most of the time. Whenever she got outside her fence, she would eat bark from the fruit trees. One time she had nipped all the buds from a budding grapevine, nearly killing the vine.

Daniel held Jenny's rope now as she frisked about and snatched mouthfuls of grass in the pasture. She was happy to go along to get the cows. Sheba trotted ahead, sniffing for mice.

The children followed the cows to the barn. Rebecca went to the calf pen right inside the barn door. Three hungry little calves looked out eagerly through the boards, waiting for their supper. Rebecca stood at the gate and called, "Come, Mama Cow! Here, Mama Cow!" A white cow with one stubby horn pushed her way through the other cows and walked straight to the calf pen. Rebecca swung the gate open and Mama Cow walked inside. Soon all the little calves were busily drinking milk.

Rebecca thought Mama Cow was a very smart cow. She came right to the calf pen when her name was called. The other cows had names too, but they did not come when they were called. They probably didn't even know what their own names were.

Rebecca and Daniel stood watching the calves finish drinking their supper, then they turned Mama Cow out of the pen. There were other chores to do. Everyone was needed when it was haying time. Mom was doing the milking tonight so Daddy could finish baling the last field, and Daniel helped her by bringing more cows into the milking parlor each time she turned some out.

After Rebecca had swept the alleyways, she and Sarah got the egg basket and searched all over the barn for eggs. It seemed the

hens were always looking for new hiding places to lay their eggs, but it was fun looking for the hiding places. Sometimes there was an egg in a corner of the twine box where the used twine was kept. Sometimes there were eggs in the calves' feeding trough or in a bucket of shelled corn by the barn wall. Today, one of the hens had found a little space just the right size for a nest behind several bales of old hay stacked in the far corner of the barn. When Rebecca reached in for the eggs, she got a vicious peck on the back of her hand. The hen was sitting on the nest! Rebecca was so startled that she jerked her hand back out. The hen fluffed her feathers and muttered, "Clook, clook, clook."

"Did that chicken peck you?" Sarah asked, wide-eyed. Rebecca showed her the spot where a little blood was seeping through the skin.

"The hen is broody," Rebecca said. "She wants to stay sitting on her eggs and hatch little chicks. But she can't sit here; it's too dangerous." Rebecca handed the egg basket to Sarah. Then quick as a flash, she put her cupped hand on top of the hen's head. It was dark under her hand, so the hen did not try to peck her. With her other hand, Rebecca got all the eggs out from under the hen. "You can't sit on a nest on the floor," she told

the hen. "Some dark night a coon could come in here and get you." The hen grumbled softly as the girls walked away to help unload more hay.

Rebecca. "You've been asking to make cheese," she said. "You may start by making this culture."

Rebecca clapped her hands. The time had finally come! Mom told her how to do each step. First she got a quart canning jar and scrubbed it in hot, soapy water. Then she filled the jar three-quarters full of fresh skim milk and screwed the lid on. She put the jar of milk in the tall kettle with a canning rack in the bottom and set the kettle on the stove. After pouring in cold water until it covered the jar, she put the lid on the kettle.

"Now we have to watch until it starts to boil, and then let it boil for thirty minutes," said Mom. "After that we'll take the whole kettle outside and let it cool to about 75 degrees."

When Rebecca dipped a thermometer into the water later that afternoon, it showed that the temperature was almost right. She lifted the jar and carried it in to the kitchen counter. "The milk is cool enough," she called.

Under Mom's supervision, she washed her hands and got a clean spoon. After carefully opening the new packet of culture, she measured out a half teaspoon of the powder and taped the packet shut. Then she unscrewed the lid of her culture milk, dumped in the culture powder, and quickly replaced the lid. Mom explained that the culture powder is a special kind of bacteria that is good in cheese. The milk in the jar had been heated to kill all other bacteria in the milk so that the good cheese bacteria would grow and multiply and make all the canned milk into more cheese culture. They had to keep the lid on the jar so no other bacteria could get in from the air.

Rebecca shook the jar to thoroughly mix the powder into the milk. A few minutes later she shook the jar again. Then they set the jar on top of the refrigerator. That was a funny place to set a jar of milk, but the warmth from the refrigerator motor kept the air up there around 75 degrees, which was a good temperature for incubating culture.

The next morning when Rebecca slowly tilted the jar to see if the culture was done, the milk inside was thick like yogurt. It was done perfectly! Now she knew how to make culture all by herself.

Mom told Rebecca to freeze the culture in ice cube trays. They would use some of it to make cheese. When they wanted to make culture again, they would use two cubes of this frozen culture. This way they would not need to buy it in the packet very often.

One evening when the children went out to the barn to chore, Jenny had a surprise for them. Two tiny kids were standing on wobbly legs in her pen! Rebecca and Daniel were so excited they could hardly get their chores done. The little kids were so cute and soft. They nickered in wee baby voices, and Jenny answered them in her big mama voice. One kid was black and gray and white like Jenny. The other was brown and white.

"I thought goats had their babies in the spring," Daniel puzzled. "All the other times we had kids in the spring."

"Most of the time goats have their babies in the springtime,"

Daddy answered, "but not always."

Jenny gave lots of good, sweet milk. Daddy decided they would milk her and then divide her milk to use for various things. Some of the milk they put into bottles and fed to the kids. Some of it would be made into cheese, and the family would drink whatever was left.

Rebecca and Daniel took turns milking Jenny and feeding the kids. The kids grew fast and were soon jumping and frisking around. Donut, the brown and white kid, was soon the bigger of the two. In a couple of days, he had little horn tips growing out of his head. The black and gray and white kid was named Amiga.

Daniel liked to lie in the soft straw and let the kids run over him. Their little hoofs felt good on his back.

"I'm afraid Amiga is sick!" Rebecca said one evening as she found Daniel washing his hands at the milk house hose. "She

didn't want to run and play like Donut. She just lay in the corner of the pen, and she hardly drank any milk."

When the children told Daddy about Amiga, he said, "Maybe she will feel better tomorrow morning and be hungry for her milk again." But in the morning Amiga was not better. Her little nose was dry and her eyes looked sad. Rebecca felt sorry for her.

"She needs water," Daddy said when he saw Amiga. "Sick animals, especially baby ones, need to keep drinking water to get better." He showed the children how to gently pinch the skin on Amiga's neck and pull it out just a little. When he let go, the skin stayed raised rather than flattening as it should have. "That means Amiga is too dry inside. You need to give her small amounts of water very often."

Mom mixed a teaspoon of corn syrup, a fourth teaspoon of baking soda, a pinch of salt, and two cups of water. Every half hour or so Rebecca warmed a little of the mixture and tried to get Amiga to drink it. At first Amiga turned her head away, but when she tasted the sweetness, she was willing to swallow a little.

Rebecca worked hard to doctor Amiga back to health. She went out just before bedtime to feed her, and the next morning she was the first one in the barn again. Amiga seemed to be just a little better.

There was a lot of work to be done that day. Daddy thought there might be frost that night, so he told the three children to take pails and a garden fork to the sweet potato patch. There they pulled the long, sprawling vines to the side and used the fork to dig deeply around the roots to pull the stout, orange sweet potatoes. Sarah gathered the broken or scratched sweet potatoes and put them in a bucket for Mom to can. All the perfect ones would be spread on newspaper to cure for a few weeks. Then each sweet potato would be wrapped in a piece of newspaper and stored in a box where it was warm.

Rebecca didn't want to go all the way from the garden to the barn to feed Amiga. So, when it was warm enough, she brought the little sick kid to a sunny place in the yard close to the garden. Amiga did not get up and follow the children when they walked past her. She lay in her sunny spot, sheltered from the chilly breeze. Sheba, good watch dog that she was, stayed nearby to be sure nothing hurt Amiga.

After dinner Daddy told the children, "Amiga's nose is too warm. I think she has a fever. She needs all the water you can get her to drink." He got a syringe with a little bit of white medicine in it and gave Amiga a shot.

That evening they fixed a box with a thick, soft bed of sawdust in it and brought Amiga into the house beside the woodstove. They mixed a little raw egg with her water mixture, and Rebecca and Mom took turns to get up every two hours to feed her.

Early in the morning when Rebecca tiptoed down the stairs, Amiga lifted her head and nickered weakly. She struggled to get up, but Rebecca helped her to stand. Amiga stretched and waggled her little tail. Rebecca laughed delightedly. "You're getting better!" she exclaimed.

Everyone rejoiced at the good news. "Amiga must be feeling better if she stretched," Daddy said. "I've never seen a very sick animal stretch." They added some more egg and a little milk to the feeding mixture, and Rebecca kept feeding her all she would drink.

"Your diligence is paying off," Mom told Rebecca. "I'm sure

Amiga would have died if you hadn't taken such good care of her."

Rebecca was glad she had cared for the kid. Now Amiga would soon be able to go out with Jenny and Donut, and jump and frisk and butt the hay in the pen. Goats like to jump up onto things, so Daniel had set a bale of old hay on end against one wall in the goat pen. It was the kids' favorite place to play, and even Jenny jumped up on it and tried to balance on the top.

When Rebecca went to the barn for chores that evening, she carried Amiga to the goat pen. The goats were all glad to see each other again. Amiga was still too weak to jump on the bale, but when Rebecca and Daniel looked in the goat pen before going to the house for supper, they saw all three goats snuggled in the corner of the pen, chewing cuds and looking sleepy.

Rebecca's heart was full of contentment and happiness. "Thank you, God, for making our little goat better," she prayed.

It was Saturday morning, December 2. At first when Rebecca woke up she couldn't remember why this was a special day. Then she threw the covers back and jumped out of bed. Of course! December 2 was her birthday! Last year she had thought it sounded big to be seven, but now eight seemed even better.

When her bed had been made as perfectly as an eight-year-old could make it, she ran down the wooden stairs. "Happy birthday!" called Mom from the stove where she was frying bacon.

"Happy birthday!" said Sarah, looking out from behind a cupboard door. "I'm setting the table for you."

"Thank you," Rebecca answered happily.

At the breakfast table, there was an envelope on Rebecca's plate. It was a birthday card, she knew, but family devotions came first. Daddy read from the Bible while they all listened quietly. Then they sang:

> Jesus bids us shine with a clear, pure light,
> Like a little candle burning in the night;
> In this world of darkness we must shine,
> You in your small corner and I in mine.

Then they all knelt to pray. Daddy prayed for Mom and for each of the children. He asked God to bless Rebecca on her birthday and to help her live for Him.

Then it was time for breakfast. Rebecca opened her card and saw on the front a picture of a cute little goat. Daddy's eyes were twinkling as if he knew a secret. Mom's eyes were twinkling too, and she said, "There is a birthday gift for you named Amiga out in the barn."

Rebecca was speechless. Amiga was now her very own pet! She could hardly believe it. "Oh, thank you!" she exclaimed.

As they ate the fried bacon with eggs and toast with butter and orange marmalade, Rebecca couldn't keep the smiles away.

That morning there was cheese to make. They had almost two gallons of Jenny's milk in the refrigerator, and Rebecca was going to make cheese from it—her birthday cheese!

Mom helped her with the things she was not big enough to do. After the cheese[1] was done, Rebecca stood admiring it in the press. "That was fun!" she said. "Now when can we eat it?"

---

[1] To see the recipe she used, see page 36.

"Your cheese is made of goat milk, so the longer it is aged, the stronger the flavor will be. It will taste best while it is fresh," Mom said.

"Let's have it for supper," Rebecca suggested.

At chore time that evening, Daniel said he would do Rebecca's barn chores because it was her birthday. That was a treat, but Rebecca still wanted to spend some time with Amiga. She sat on a hay bale and let the kids butt her knees and jump on her shoulders. Amiga stood for a while on the bale beside Rebecca. Then she climbed into Rebecca's lap and lay down. Rebecca smoothed the goat's silky hair and smiled. Amiga had grown fond of her when she had tried so hard to help her get well again.

After a while Rebecca carefully put the sleepy kid back on the floor and went to help finish up the chores. It was going to be a cold, windy night, so all the barn doors and the hay hole covers must be closed. Rebecca walked around with Daddy and Daniel to all the calf pens and along the rows of cows to make sure each one was comfortable and warm. Sheba lifted her nose from her paws, and her tail gave one sleepy wag when they passed the heap of hay that was her bed.

"Listen," said Daddy. They stood still for a moment. All over the barn was the soft rustle of hay being eaten by the animals. No other noise was heard. It was a peaceful, satisfied sound. Daddy closed the walkway gate and turned off the lights. "All is snug in the barn," he said. "Now we can go in for supper."

There was candlelight at the supper table that evening. The

platter of fried cheese sandwiches and the bowl of thick bean soup looked delicious. "Bean soup and cheese sandwiches!" Rebecca cheered. "That's my favorite supper."

"Your cheese turned out very nicely," Mom told Rebecca as they passed the platter around after prayer.

"These sandwiches look delicious," Daddy agreed.

The cold wind was complaining loudly outside the corners of the house, trying to find cracks to get inside. But in the kitchen it was cozy and warm. Rebecca looked around in the soft candlelight at her loving family, and her heart was so full of happiness it almost hurt.

I think I'm the happiest girl in the whole world! she thought, as she picked up her toasty sandwich and took a bite. *God gave me so many good things: parents who love me, a fun and helpful brother and sister, and a little pet all my own. I want to do my best to please God always.*

COLBY CHEESE

2 gallons goat milk (if using cow milk, double the recipe; otherwise the cheese will dry out too quickly as it ages)
6 tablespoons prepared mesophilic culture
1 teaspoon liquid rennet, or ¼ rennet tablet, crushed
¼ cup water
2 tablespoons non-iodized salt

Warm the milk to 90°F. Add a small amount of the warm milk to the culture and stir until smooth, then pour it into the cheese milk and mix thoroughly. Cover and let the milk ripen for an hour.

Stir the rennet into the water and rewarm the milk, if necessary, to 86°F. Pour rennet mixture slowly into milk while stirring, and continue to stir gently for 3 minutes. Put the lid back on, set the pan on a folded towel and cover with another towel. Let it set 30 minutes, or until the curd breaks clean over a knife blade stuck in sideways.

Cut the curd into 3/8" cubes. Stir gently, bringing the bottom curds up to the top. Slowly heat the curds, two degrees every five minutes, until the temperature reaches 102°F, stirring all the time. Keep the temperature at 102°F for 30 minutes, keeping the bottom curds stirred to the top.

Drain off the whey to the level of the curds, and add 60°F water to the curds, stirring gently, until the temperature of the curds and water reaches 80°F. Keep the temperature at 80°F for 15 minutes, stirring occasionally.

Pour the curds into a cheesecloth-lined colander and drain for 20 minutes. Break the curds apart into thumbnail size pieces, add the salt, and mix thoroughly.

Put the salted curds into a cheesecloth-lined cheese press or cheese mold and press at 20 pounds of pressure for 20 minutes.

Take the cheese from the mold, gently peel away the cheesecloth, turn the cheese over, re-dress it and press at 30 pounds pressure for 20 minutes.

Repeat the process but press at 40 pounds pressure for 12 hours.

Remove the cheese from the press and peel off the cheesecloth. Place the cheese on a clean, folded tea towel and let it dry at room temperature for several hours. Turn the cheese on its other side on another clean, dry tea towel. Continue turning the cheese from side to side on a fresh towel as often as the towels get damp.

Goat milk cheese should be eaten right away. If cheese is made with cow milk, follow instructions below:

In a few days, when the cheese is dry to the touch, coat with cheese wax or brush with olive oil to seal it and store in a drawer in the refrigerator to age for 2–3 months. The cheese should be turned over onto a fresh towel every couple of days.

Note: If you make your own culture, and the culture does not get thick in 12 hours, try keeping it at 85 degrees instead of 75 degrees.

About the Author and Artist

AUTHOR
Valerie Miller
ARTIST
Charity Miller

Valerie and Charity Miller are sisters living in rural Honesdale, Pennsylvania. They live with their parents and three other siblings, and belong to the Carley Brook Church. They thoroughly enjoyed growing up on a farm and learning to make cheese and do other old-fashioned arts that are becoming lost today.